THE VEGETARIAN DASH DIET COOKBOOK

The Comprehensive Guide to Nutrient Packed Recipes to Naturally Reduce Blood Pressure and Live a Healthier Life

SUSAN VICTORIA

TABLE OF CONTENT

INTRODUCTION

In a world where health is wealth and dietary choices are paramount, the fusion of two powerful dietary approaches brings forth a groundbreaking concept: The Vegetarian DASH Diet. Imagine a culinary journey that harmoniously marries the principles of vegetarianism with the proven advantages of the Dietary Approaches to Stop Hypertension (DASH) diet. This is not merely a cookbook; it is a transformative experience waiting to tantalize taste buds and revolutionize your well-being.

The Vegetarian DASH Diet, at its core, is a celebration of wholesome nourishment that transcends dietary boundaries. It embraces the bounties of plant-based ingredients while upholding the essence of DASH – a dietary approach acknowledged by health experts for its effectiveness in lowering blood pressure and promoting heart health. But here's the twist: no longer are you confined to animal products to achieve these health goals. The union of these two approaches opens a door to a realm where flavor knows no bounds, and where health benefits are as diverse as the colorful spectrum of fruits and vegetables.

Brimming with benefits that cater to both your body and taste palate, the Vegetarian DASH Diet brings you a compendium of advantages that extend beyond the surface. Picture savoring dishes that reduce the risk of chronic illnesses, enhance weight management, and elevate your energy levels – all while relishing in the delightful symphony of textures and flavors. This is a diet crafted to not only nurture your physical health but also elevate your culinary encounters to a whole new echelon.

As you embark on this culinary expedition within the pages of this cookbook, you can anticipate a treasure trove of recipes that harmonize simplicity with gastronomic excellence. From vibrant breakfast options that greet your mornings with zest, to sumptuous lunches that fuel your afternoons, and decadent dinners that transform evenings into gourmet celebrations – the array of recipes promises to cater to every craving and occasion.

But this cookbook is more than a collection of recipes; it's your trusted culinary companion. Prepare to unravel the secrets behind ingredient substitutions that uphold the DASH principles without compromising on taste. Discover cooking techniques that preserve both flavor and nutrients, making each bite not just a delight but also a step towards vitality. And as you navigate this culinary voyage, you'll find yourself equipped with insights into meal planning, grocery shopping, and embracing a sustainable approach to your newfound dietary lifestyle.

In the pages that follow, be prepared to witness the fusion of two dietary realms into a tapestry of flavor and vitality. The Vegetarian DASH Diet cookbook is your gateway to a world where health-consciousness dances with epicurean pleasures. So, turn the page and step into a realm where every meal is an act of self-care and a celebration of the art of nourishment.

CHAPTER ONE: UNDERSTANDING DASH DIET AND VEGETARIAN DASH DIET

The **DASH (Dietary Approaches to Stop Hypertension)** diet is a dietary plan that holds a prominent place in the realm of nutrition, acclaimed for its remarkable impact on promoting heart health, managing blood pressure, and fostering overall well-being. Devised by the **National Heart, Lung, and Blood Institute (NHLBI),** the DASH diet originated as a response to the increasing prevalence of hypertension and cardiovascular diseases. Rooted in the fundamental understanding of how dietary choices profoundly influence health, the DASH diet embodies a balanced approach that transcends mere weight loss; it advocates for a lifelong commitment to a nutrient-rich lifestyle.

At its core, the DASH diet resonates with the philosophy of choosing foods that align with nature's bounty. **Fruits and vegetables** emerge as the unsung heroes, gracing the plate with vibrant colors that signify a treasure trove of vitamins, minerals, and antioxidants. These essential nutrients not only fortify the body's defense against illnesses but also contribute to the vitality that accompanies optimal health.

In essence, the DASH diet underscores the importance of embracing the inherent benefits of whole, unprocessed foods.

Whole grains constitute another cornerstone of the DASH diet. These grains, such as brown rice, whole wheat, and quinoa, furnish complex carbohydrates and dietary fiber that are instrumental in steadying blood sugar levels and supporting digestive health. The DASH diet's advocacy for whole grains mirrors its commitment to nourishing the body holistically, beyond the narrow confines of lowering blood pressure.

Lean protein sources, the diet's third pillar, encompass an array of options like poultry, fish, beans, lentils, and nuts. These sources, rich in essential amino acids, lend themselves to the sustenance of muscle mass while offering an alternative to high-saturated-fat meats. The DASH diet's reverence for protein selection underscores its holistic outlook that encompasses both cardiovascular health and overall well-being.

A defining feature of the DASH diet is its call for **restraint in sodium consumption**. In a world where processed and packaged foods reign, sodium often permeates the modern diet. The DASH diet, however, advocates for a paradigm shift that privileges the flavors of nature's bounty. This entails the strategic use of herbs, spices, and other natural seasonings to elevate the culinary experience while minimizing reliance on excessive salt. This aspect of the diet is testament to its thoughtful approach that transcends mere health benefits to encompass sensory delight.

In addition to dietary considerations, the DASH diet embraces a multifaceted lifestyle. Regular physical activity, stress management, and abstaining from smoking are woven into the fabric of this approach. The DASH diet recognizes that true health is a synergy of various components, each contributing to the harmonious symphony of vitality.

Moreover, the DASH diet isn't a rigid formula; it's adaptable to diverse dietary preferences. For those with lactose tolerance, dairy products provide essential calcium and vitamin D. Meanwhile, for individuals who eschew animal products, the Vegetarian DASH diet offers an avenue to harness its benefits while adhering to their chosen lifestyle.

The legacy of the DASH diet lies in its transformative potential. From a reduction in blood pressure to improvements in cholesterol profiles, the diet extends its reach beyond the individual to shape public health initiatives. Its principles, simple yet profound, offer a blueprint for those seeking to foster lasting well-being.

Its emphasis on whole, nutrient-rich foods, controlled sodium intake, and the intertwining of dietary choices with broader health considerations distinguishes it as a holistic approach to well-being. By steering individuals toward a harmonious relationship with nature's bounty, the DASH diet serves as a beacon of health in a world often overshadowed by processed indulgence. It's a testament to the profound impact that dietary choices wield on human health and, consequently, the quality of life.

What Is a Vegetarian DASH DIET?

The Vegetarian DASH (Dietary Approaches to Stop Hypertension) diet is a plant-based adaptation of the original DASH diet, which aims to promote heart health, lower blood pressure, and reduce the risk of cardiovascular diseases. Unlike the standard DASH diet, the Vegetarian DASH diet eliminates meat and fish, prioritizing plant-based sources of nutrients. Here's a closer look at its key components:

The foundation of the Vegetarian DASH diet is built upon plant-based foods, including fruits, vegetables, whole grains, legumes, nuts, seeds, and plant-based protein sources.

Protein intake is maintained through plant-based substitutes such as beans, lentils, chickpeas, tofu, tempeh, seitan, quinoa, nuts, and seeds, as meat and fish are excluded.

Dairy products or their alternatives play a role in providing calcium and vitamin D. Lacto-vegetarian versions might include low-fat or fat-free dairy, while vegan versions utilize fortified plant-based milk alternatives.

Whole grains remain central to the Vegetarian DASH diet, offering complex carbohydrates and fiber. Brown rice, whole wheat pasta, quinoa, oats, and whole grain bread are staples.

The focus on nutrient density is preserved, ensuring that the diet supplies essential vitamins, minerals, and antioxidants from plant sources.

Sodium intake is limited, requiring the avoidance of high-sodium processed foods and the utilization of natural seasonings to enhance flavors.

Healthy fats sourced from avocados, nuts, seeds, and olive oil contribute to heart health and satiety.

Portion control remains crucial for managing calorie intake and promoting a healthy weight, even within a plant-based context.

Sugary foods and drinks are restricted, with an emphasis on the inherent sweetness of fruits.

The Vegetarian DASH diet is adaptable to various vegetarian preferences, such as lacto-vegetarian, ovo-vegetarian, and vegan variations.

Balanced nutritional intake of macronutrients (carbohydrates, proteins, and fats) and micronutrients (vitamins and minerals) supports overall health.

By embracing whole, plant-based foods and minimizing animal products, the Vegetarian DASH diet provides a heart-healthy approach for individuals following vegetarian lifestyles. It has been associated with benefits like improved blood pressure, better cholesterol profiles, and reduced risk of chronic diseases.

Benefits of a Vegetarian DASH Diet?

The Vegetarian Dietary Approaches to Stop Hypertension (DASH) diet offers a range of health benefits due to its focus on nutrient-rich plant-based foods and reduced intake of processed foods and meats. Here are some of the key benefits of following a Vegetarian DASH diet:

1. Blood Pressure Management: The DASH diet was originally designed to help manage and lower blood pressure. By emphasizing fruits, vegetables, whole grains, nuts, seeds, and legumes while limiting sodium intake, the Vegetarian DASH diet can contribute to better blood pressure control.

2. Heart Health: The diet's emphasis on plant-based foods naturally leads to lower saturated fat and cholesterol intake. This can lead to a reduction in the risk of heart disease and related conditions like heart attacks and strokes.

3. Weight Management: The diet's focus on whole, fiber-rich foods can help with weight management. Plant-based foods are generally lower in calories while being more filling due to their high fiber content.

4. Improved Digestion: The Vegetarian DASH diet, rich in fiber from fruits, vegetables, and whole grains, can promote healthy digestion and regular bowel movements.

5. Reduced Risk of Chronic Diseases: By prioritizing nutrient-dense foods, the Vegetarian DASH diet can help reduce the risk of chronic diseases such as type 2 diabetes, certain types of cancer, and obesity.

6. Balanced Nutrition: The diet encourages a balanced intake of a wide range of nutrients. By incorporating various plant-based foods, individuals are more likely to meet their nutritional needs, including vitamins, minerals, and antioxidants.

7. Lowered Risk of Kidney Stones: The Vegetarian DASH diet's focus on adequate fluid intake and plant-based foods can reduce the risk of developing kidney stones.

8. Better Blood Sugar Control: With its emphasis on complex carbohydrates, fiber, and whole foods, the diet can contribute to better blood sugar control, making it beneficial for individuals with or at risk of type 2 diabetes.

9. Improved Gut Health: The inclusion of plant-based foods like fruits, vegetables, and legumes provides prebiotic fiber that supports a healthy gut microbiome.

10. Sustainability: Choosing a plant-based diet can have positive environmental impacts by reducing the demand for animal agriculture and its associated resource use.

11. Long-Term Health: The Vegetarian DASH diet's focus on whole foods and balanced nutrition promotes overall health and well-being, which can contribute to a higher quality of life as you age.

12. Variety and Flavor: A well-executed Vegetarian DASH diet offers a wide variety of flavors, textures, and cuisines, making it a flavorful and enjoyable way to eat.

Tips for Success on the Vegetarian DASH Diet

Here are some tips to help you succeed on the Vegetarian DASH Diet:

1. Educate Yourself: Understand the core principles of the Vegetarian DASH Diet. Learn about the types of foods to emphasize and limit, as well as the recommended nutrient intake.

2. Plan Your Meals: Take time to plan your meals for the week. This will help you make balanced choices and reduce the temptation to opt for less healthy options when you're hungry.

3. Embrace Whole Foods: Focus on whole, unprocessed foods. Choose whole grains, fresh fruits, vegetables, nuts, seeds, and legumes for nutrient-rich meals.

4. Portion Control: Pay attention to portion sizes to avoid overeating. Use measuring cups, scales, and visual cues to gauge appropriate serving sizes.

5. Monitor Sodium Intake: Be mindful of your sodium intake, as excessive salt consumption can counteract the diet's benefits for blood pressure. Choose low-sodium or no-salt-added options when possible.

6. Include a Variety of Vegetables: Incorporate a wide range of colorful vegetables into your meals to ensure you're getting a diverse array of nutrients and antioxidants.

7. Get Creative with Protein: Experiment with plant-based protein sources like beans, lentils, tofu, tempeh, quinoa, and nuts. These foods will help you meet your protein needs without relying on meat.

8. Prioritize Healthy Fats: Include sources of healthy fats, such as avocados, nuts, seeds, and olive oil. These fats support heart health and overall well-being.

9. Opt for Whole Grains: Choose whole grains over refined grains. Quinoa, brown rice, whole wheat, and oats are excellent choices that provide fiber and sustained energy.

10. Read Labels: When buying packaged foods, read labels to identify hidden sources of added sugars and high sodium content. Look for products with minimal processing.

11. Stay Hydrated: Drink plenty of water throughout the day. Herbal teas and infused water can also be refreshing options.

12. Prepare Your Own Meals: Cooking at home gives you control over ingredients and preparation methods, making it easier to stick to the diet's guidelines.

13. Snack Wisely: Keep healthy snacks on hand to prevent reaching for unhealthy options when hunger strikes. Opt for raw veggies, fruit, unsalted nuts, or yogurt.

14. Limit Added Sugars: Minimize your consumption of sugary foods and beverages. Focus on naturally sweet foods like fruits and use alternatives like honey or maple syrup sparingly.

15. Manage Stress: Incorporate stress-reduction techniques like meditation, yoga, deep breathing, or hobbies to support your overall well-being.

16. Listen to Your Body: Pay attention to your body's hunger and fullness cues. Eat slowly and mindfully to avoid overeating.

17. Be Patient: Sustainable changes take time. Don't expect immediate results. Focus on the positive impact you're making on your health.

18. Seek Support: Enlist the support of friends, family, or a support group to stay motivated and share experiences.

19. Monitor Progress: Keep track of your progress, whether it's improvements in blood pressure, energy levels, weight, or overall health.

20. Consult a Professional: If you have specific health concerns or nutritional needs, consider consulting a registered dietitian or healthcare professional for personalized guidance.

Remember, the key to success on any diet is consistency, moderation, and making choices that align with your health goals. It's about building a sustainable lifestyle that supports your well-being.

How to Use This Cookbook

Here's a guide on how to use the Vegetarian DASH Diet cookbook effectively:

1. Introduction:

Start by reading the introduction section to understand the purpose and benefits of the Vegetarian DASH Diet. Familiarize yourself with the key principles of the diet and how it aligns with your health goals.

2. Table of Contents:

Browse through the table of contents to get an overview of the recipes and chapters included in the cookbook.

3. Chapter Overview:

Before diving into the recipes, read the introductory sections of each chapter. This will provide you with insights into the types of dishes you'll find and the nutritional focus of each chapter.

4. Recipe Selection:

Select recipes based on your preferences, dietary needs, and goals. If you're new to the Vegetarian DASH Diet, consider starting with recipes from the "Basics of the Vegetarian DASH Diet" chapter to build a strong foundation.

5. Meal Planning:

Plan your meals for the week using the cookbook. Look for a balanced variety of recipes that include breakfasts, lunches, dinners, and snacks. The "Meal Plans and Tips" chapter might have pre-made meal plans to follow. A sample 4 weeks meal plan is included in chapter 2 of this book

6. Grocery List:

Check the ingredient lists of the recipes you've chosen and create a shopping list. Organize it based on sections of the grocery store to make your shopping trip efficient.

7. Cooking Instructions:

Follow the detailed cooking instructions provided for each recipe. Pay attention to any special techniques or tips mentioned to ensure the best results.

8. Portion Control:

Be mindful of portion sizes to ensure you're following the recommended guidelines for the Vegetarian DASH Diet. Consider using measuring tools or referencing serving sizes mentioned in the cookbook.

9. Experiment and Customize:

Feel free to get creative with the recipes. Add or substitute ingredients according to your taste preferences and dietary needs. The recipes are a starting point; make them your own!

10. Meal Diversity:

Rotate through different recipes to ensure you're getting a variety of nutrients and flavors. This also helps prevent dietary monotony.

11. Gradual Incorporation:

If you're new to the Vegetarian DASH Diet, consider gradually incorporating its principles into your routine. Start by replacing a few meals per week with DASH-friendly recipes and gradually increase over time.

12. Tracking Progress:

As you continue with the diet, track your progress in terms of how you feel, any changes in health indicators (like blood pressure), and your overall well-being.

13. Seeking Professional Guidance:

If you have specific health concerns or goals, consider consulting a registered dietitian or healthcare professional. They can provide personalized advice and help tailor the diet to your individual needs.

Remember, the cookbook is a tool to help you make delicious and nutritious meals that align with the Vegetarian DASH Diet principles. Feel free to enjoy the journey of exploring new flavors and discovering the positive impact this diet can have on your health.

CHAPTER TWO

28-DAY MEAL PLAN

Week 1:
Day 1:

- **Breakfast**: Quinoa Breakfast Bowl

- **Lunch**: Chickpea and Vegetable Stir-Fry

- **Dinner**: Stuffed Bell Peppers with Quinoa and Black Beans

- **Snack**: Carrot and Celery Sticks with Hummus

- **Dessert**: Mixed Berry Parfait with Greek Yogurt

- **Smoothie**: Green Power Smoothie with Spinach and Banana

Day 2:

- **Breakfast:** Greek Yogurt Parfait

- **Lunch:** Spinach and Quinoa Salad

- **Dinner**: Spaghetti Squash with Marinara Sauce and Steamed Broccoli

- **Snack**: Greek Yogurt with Mixed Berries

- **Dessert**: Baked Apples with Cinnamon and Walnuts

- **Smoothie:** Berry Blast Smoothie with Mixed Berries and Almond Milk

Day 3:

- **Breakfast**: Veggie Omelette

- **Lunch:** Lentil Soup with Whole Wheat Roll

- **Dinner:** Tofu and Vegetable Stir-Fry with Brown Rice

- **Snack:** Air-Popped Popcorn with Herbs and Spices

- **Dessert:** Chia Seed Pudding with Fresh Fruit

- **Smoothie**: Tropical Paradise Smoothie with Pineapple, Mango, and Coconut Water

Day 4:

- **Breakfast**: Overnight Chia Pudding

- **Lunch:** Hummus and Veggie Wrap

- **Dinner**: Mushroom and Spinach Stuffed Portobello Mushrooms

- **Snack**: Almonds and Walnuts Mix

- **Dessert:** Dark Chocolate-Dipped Strawberries

- **Smoothie**: Creamy Avocado Smoothie with Lime and Honey

Day 5:

- **Breakfast**: Whole Wheat Pancakes

- **Lunch**: Brown Rice and Black Bean Bowl

- **Dinner**: Roasted Vegetable and Chickpea Salad

- **Snack**: Sliced Cucumber with Cottage Cheese

- **Dessert**: Mango Sorbet with Mint Leaves

- **Smoothie**: Peanut Butter Banana Smoothie with Greek Yogurt

Day 6:

- **Breakfast**: Avocado Toast with Tomato

- **Lunch**: Caprese Salad with Balsamic Glaze

- **Dinner**: Cauliflower and Lentil Curry with Whole Wheat Naan

- **Snack**: Rice Cakes with Peanut Butter and Banana Slices

- **Dessert**: Oatmeal Raisin Cookies (using whole wheat flour and less sugar)

- **Smoothie**: Cucumber Mint Cooler Smoothie

Day 7:

- **Breakfast**: Berry and Nut Oatmeal

- **Lunch**: Roasted Vegetable and Couscous Medley

- **Dinner:** Zucchini Noodles with Pesto and Cherry Tomatoes

- **Snack**: Veggie Chips (Baked Zucchini, Sweet Potato, or Kale)

- **Dessert:** Fruit Salad with Honey-Lime Drizzle

- **Smoothie**: Oatmeal and Almond Smoothie with Dates and Cinnamon

Day 8:

- **Breakfast**: Quinoa Breakfast Bowl

- **Lunch:** Chickpea and Vegetable Stir-Fry

- **Dinner:** Stuffed Bell Peppers with Quinoa and Black Beans

- **Snack:** Carrot and Celery Sticks with Hummus

- **Dessert:** Mixed Berry Parfait with Greek Yogurt

- Smoothie: Green Power Smoothie with Spinach and Banana

Day 9:

- **Breakfast**: Greek Yogurt Parfait

- **Lunch:** Spinach and Quinoa Salad

- **Dinner**: Spaghetti Squash with Marinara Sauce and Steamed Broccoli

- **Snack**: Greek Yogurt with Mixed Berries

- **Dessert:** Baked Apples with Cinnamon and Walnuts

- **Smoothie**: Berry Blast Smoothie with Mixed Berries and Almond Milk

Day 10:

- **Breakfast**: Veggie Omelette

- **Lunch**: Lentil Soup with Whole Wheat Roll

- **Dinner**: Tofu and Vegetable Stir-Fry with Brown Rice

- **Snack**: Air-Popped Popcorn with Herbs and Spices

- **Dessert**: Chia Seed Pudding with Fresh Fruit

- **Smoothie**: Tropical Paradise Smoothie with Pineapple, Mango, and Coconut Water

Day 11:

- **Breakfast:** Overnight Chia Pudding

- **Lunch**: Hummus and Veggie Wrap

- **Dinner**: Mushroom and Spinach Stuffed Portobello Mushrooms

- **Snack**: Almonds and Walnuts Mix

- **Dessert**: Dark Chocolate-Dipped Strawberries

- **Smoothie**: Creamy Avocado Smoothie with Lime and Honey

Day 12:

- **Breakfast**: Whole Wheat Pancakes

- **Lunch:** Brown Rice and Black Bean Bowl

- **Dinner:** Roasted Vegetable and Chickpea Salad

- **Snack**: Sliced Cucumber with Cottage Cheese

- **Dessert:** Mango Sorbet with Mint Leaves

- **Smoothie**: Peanut Butter Banana Smoothie with Greek Yogurt

Day 13:

- **Breakfast**: Avocado Toast with Tomato

- **Lunch**: Caprese Salad with Balsamic Glaze

- **Dinner**: Cauliflower and Lentil Curry with Whole Wheat Naan

- **Snack**: Rice Cakes with Peanut Butter and Banana Slices

- **Dessert**: Oatmeal Raisin Cookies (using whole wheat flour and less sugar)

- **Smoothie**: Cucumber Mint Cooler Smoothie

Day 14:

- **Breakfast**: Berry and Nut Oatmeal

- **Lunch:** Roasted Vegetable and Couscous Medley

- **Dinner**: Zucchini Noodles with Pesto and Cherry Tomatoes

- **Snack:** Veggie Chips (Baked Zucchini, Sweet Potato, or Kale)

- **Dessert**: Fruit Salad with Honey-Lime Drizzle

- **Smoothie**: Oatmeal and Almond Smoothie with Dates and Cinnamon

Day 15:

- **Breakfast**: Quinoa Breakfast Bowl

- **Lunch**: Chickpea and Vegetable Stir-Fry

- **Dinner:** Stuffed Bell Peppers with Quinoa and Black Beans

- **Snack**: Carrot and Celery Sticks with Hummus

- **Dessert**: Mixed Berry Parfait with Greek Yogurt

- **Smoothie**: Green Power Smoothie with Spinach and Banana

Day 16:

- **Breakfast**: Greek Yogurt Parfait

- **Lunch:** Spinach and Quinoa Salad

- **Dinner:** Spaghetti Squash with Marinara Sauce and Steamed Broccoli

- **Snack:** Greek Yogurt with Mixed Berries

- **Dessert**: Baked Apples with Cinnamon and Walnuts

- **Smoothie:** Berry Blast Smoothie with Mixed Berries and Almond Milk

Day 17:

- **Breakfast**: Veggie Omelette

- **Lunch:** Lentil Soup with Whole Wheat Roll

- **Dinner:** Tofu and Vegetable Stir-Fry with Brown Rice

- **Snack**: Air-Popped Popcorn with Herbs and Spices

- **Dessert**: Chia Seed Pudding with Fresh Fruit

- **Smoothie:** Tropical Paradise Smoothie with Pineapple, Mango, and Coconut Water

Day 18:

- **Breakfast**: Overnight Chia Pudding

- **Lunch:** Hummus and Veggie Wrap

- **Dinner**: Mushroom and Spinach Stuffed Portobello Mushrooms

- **Snack**: Almonds and Walnuts Mix

- **Dessert**: Dark Chocolate-Dipped Strawberries

- **Smoothie**: Creamy Avocado Smoothie with Lime and Honey

Day 19:

- **Breakfast:** Whole Wheat Pancakes

- **Lunch**: Brown Rice and Black Bean Bowl

- **Dinner**: Roasted Vegetable and Chickpea Salad

- **Snack**: Sliced Cucumber with Cottage Cheese

- **Dessert:** Mango Sorbet with Mint Leaves

- **Smoothie**: Peanut Butter Banana Smoothie with Greek Yogurt

Day 20:

- **Breakfast**: Avocado Toast with Tomato

- **Lunch:** Caprese Salad with Balsamic Glaze

- **Dinner**: Cauliflower and Lentil Curry with Whole Wheat Naan

- **Snack:** Rice Cakes with Peanut Butter and Banana Slices

- **Dessert:** Oatmeal Raisin Cookies (using whole wheat flour and less sugar)

- **Smoothie**: Cucumber Mint Cooler Smoothie

Day 21:

- **Breakfast:** Berry and Nut Oatmeal

- **Lunch**: Roasted Vegetable and Couscous Medley

- **Dinner**: Zucchini Noodles with Pesto and Cherry Tomatoes

- **Snack**: Veggie Chips (Baked Zucchini, Sweet Potato, or Kale)

- **Dessert:** Fruit Salad with Honey-Lime Drizzle

- **Smoothie:** Oatmeal and Almond Smoothie with Dates and Cinnamon

Day 22:

- **Breakfast:** Quinoa Breakfast Bowl

- **Lunch**: Chickpea and Vegetable Stir-Fry

- **Dinner:** Stuffed Bell Peppers with Quinoa and Black Beans

- **Snack**: Carrot and Celery Sticks with Hummus

- **Dessert**: Mixed Berry Parfait with Greek Yogurt

- **Smoothie**: Green Power Smoothie with Spinach and Banana

Day 23:

- **Breakfast**: Greek Yogurt Parfait

- **Lunch:** Spinach and Quinoa Salad

- **Dinner:** Spaghetti Squash with Marinara Sauce and Steamed Broccoli

- **Snack:** Greek Yogurt with Mixed Berries

- **Dessert:** Baked Apples with Cinnamon and Walnuts

- **Smoothie:** Berry Blast Smoothie with Mixed Berries and Almond Milk

Day 24:

- **Breakfast**: Veggie Omelette

- **Lunch:** Lentil Soup with Whole Wheat Roll

- **Dinner:** Tofu and Vegetable Stir-Fry with Brown Rice

- **Snack**: Air-Popped Popcorn with Herbs and Spices

- **Dessert**: Chia Seed Pudding with Fresh Fruit

- **Smoothie:** Tropical Paradise Smoothie with Pineapple, Mango, and Coconut Water

Day 25:

- **Breakfast**: Overnight Chia Pudding

- **Lunch:** Hummus and Veggie Wrap

- **Dinner**: Mushroom and Spinach Stuffed Portobello Mushrooms

- **Snack**: Almonds and Walnuts Mix

- **Dessert**: Dark Chocolate-Dipped Strawberries

- **Smoothie**: Creamy Avocado Smoothie with Lime and Honey

Day 26:

- **Breakfast:** Whole Wheat Pancakes

- **Lunch**: Brown Rice and Black Bean Bowl

- **Dinner**: Roasted Vegetable and Chickpea Salad

- **Snack:** Sliced Cucumber with Cottage Cheese

- **Dessert**: Mango Sorbet with Mint Leaves

- **Smoothie**: Peanut Butter Banana Smoothie with Greek Yogurt

Day 27:

- **Breakfast**: Avocado Toast with Tomato

- **Lunch:** Caprese Salad with Balsamic Glaze

- **Dinner**: Cauliflower and Lentil Curry with Whole Wheat Naan

- **Snack**: Rice Cakes with Peanut Butter and Banana Slices

- **Dessert**: Oatmeal Raisin Cookies (using whole wheat flour and less sugar)

- **Smoothie**: Cucumber Mint Cooler Smoothie

Day 28:

- **Breakfast**: Berry and Nut Oatmeal

- **Lunch:** Roasted Vegetable and Couscous Medley

- **Dinner**: Zucchini Noodles with Pesto and Cherry Tomatoes

- **Snack**: Veggie Chips (Baked Zucchini, Sweet Potato, or Kale)

- **Dessert**: Fruit Salad with Honey-Lime Drizzle

- **Smoothie**: Oatmeal and Almond Smoothie with Dates and Cinnamon

Quinoa Breakfast Bowl:

Ingredients:
- 1 cup cooked quinoa
- 1/2 cup mixed berries (blueberries, strawberries, raspberries)
- 1 tablespoon chopped nuts (almonds, walnuts, etc.)
- 1 tablespoon honey or maple syrup
- 1/2 cup Greek yogurt

Method:

1. In a neat bowl, layer the cooked quinoa.

2. Top with mixed berries and chopped nuts.

3. Drizzle honey or maple syrup over the top.

4. Add a dollop of Greek yogurt.

5. Mix together before eating.

Servings: 1

Preparation Time: 10 minutes

Greek Yogurt Parfait:

Ingredients:

- 1/2 cup Greek yogurt

- 1/4 cup granola

- 1/4 cup mixed fresh fruits (berries, kiwi, etc.)

- 1 tablespoon honey or agave syrup

Method:

1. In a glass, layer neatly Greek yogurt.

2. Add a layer of granola and mixed fruits.

3. Drizzle honey or agave syrup over the top.

Servings: 1

Preparation Time: 5 minutes

Veggie Omelette:

Ingredients:
- 2 large eggs
- Salt and pepper to taste
- 1/4 cup diced bell peppers
- 1/4 cup diced tomatoes
- 1/4 cup chopped spinach
- 1/4 cup shredded cheese (optional)

Method:
1. In a bowl, whisk eggs and season with salt and pepper.
2. Heat a non-stick pan over medium heat and add a little oil or butter.
3. Pour in the whisked eggs.
4. Sprinkle bell peppers, tomatoes, and spinach over one half of the eggs.
5. If using cheese, sprinkle it over the veggies.
6. When the eggs are set, fold the other half over the veggies and cheese.
7. Cook until the omelette is fully set.

Servings: 1
Preparation Time: 10 minutes

Overnight Chia Pudding:

Ingredients:
- 3 tablespoons chia seeds
- 1 cup almond milk (or any milk of choice)
- 1 tablespoon honey or maple syrup
- 1/2 teaspoon vanilla extract
- Fresh fruits for topping

Method:
1. In a jar, mix chia seeds, almond milk, honey or maple syrup, and vanilla extract.
2. Stir well, making sure there are no clumps.
3. Cover the jar and refrigerate overnight.
4. In the morning, give it a good stir and top with fresh fruits.

Servings: 1
Preparation Time: 5 minutes (plus overnight refrigeration)

Whole Wheat Pancakes:

Ingredients:
- 1 cup whole wheat flour

- 1 tablespoon baking powder

- 1 tablespoon honey or maple syrup

- 1 cup milk (dairy or non-dairy)

- 1 egg

- 1 tablespoon melted butter or oil

Method:

1. In a bowl, whisk together flour, baking powder, and a pinch of salt.

2. In another bowl, mix honey or maple syrup, milk, egg, and melted butter or oil.

3. Combine wet and dry ingredients, mixing until just combined.

4. Heat a non-stick pan over medium heat and pour batter to make pancakes.

5. Cook till bubbles form on the surface, then turn and cook until golden brown.

Servings: 2-3
Preparation Time: 20 minutes

Avocado Toast with Tomato:

Ingredients:

- 1 ripe avocado
- 2 slices whole wheat bread, toasted
- 1 tomato, sliced
- Salt and pepper to taste
- Red pepper flakes (optional)

Method:

1. Mash avocado in a bowl and season with salt and pepper.
2. Spread the mashed avocado on the toasted bread slices.
3. Top with sliced tomatoes.
4. Sprinkle red pepper flakes if desired.

Servings: 1

Preparation Time: 10 minutes

Ingredients:

- 1/2 cup rolled oats
- 1 cup water or milk (dairy or non-dairy)
- 1/4 cup mixed berries
- 1 tablespoon chopped nuts (almonds, walnuts, etc.)
- 1 tablespoon honey or maple syrup

Method:

1. In a saucepan, let water or milk to a boil.
2. Add rolled oats and reduce heat to a simmer.
3. Cook until oats are creamy and tender, stirring occasionally.
4. Stir in mixed berries and chopped nuts.
5. Drizzle honey or maple syrup on top.

Servings: 1
Preparation Time: 10 minutes

Chickpea and Vegetable Stir-Fry:

Ingredients:

- 1 cup cooked chickpeas
- 1 cup mixed vegetables (bell peppers, broccoli, carrots, etc.)
- 2 tablespoons soy sauce
- 1 tablespoon olive oil
- 1 teaspoon minced garlic
- Salt and pepper to taste

Method:

1. Heat olive oil in a pan over medium-high heat.
2. Add minced garlic and sauté until fragrant.
3. Add mixed vegetables and stir-fry until slightly tender.
4. Add cooked chickpeas and soy sauce.
5. Season with salt and pepper.
6. Stir-fry for a few more minutes until everything is heated through.

Servings: 2
Preparation Time: 15 minutes

Ingredients:

- 1 cup cooked quinoa
- 2 cups fresh baby spinach
- 1/2 cup cherry tomatoes, halved
- 1/4 cup crumbled feta cheese
- 2 tablespoons balsamic vinegar
- 1 tablespoon olive oil
- Salt and pepper to taste

Method:

1. In a large bowl, combine cooked quinoa, baby spinach, cherry tomatoes, and feta cheese.
2. In a small bowl, whisk together balsamic vinegar, olive oil, salt, and pepper.
3. Drizzle the dressing over the salad and mix to combine.

Servings: 2

Preparation Time: 20 minutes

Lentil Soup with Whole Wheat Roll:

Ingredients:
- 1 cup dried green or brown lentils
- 1 onion, chopped
- 2 carrots, chopped
- 2 celery stalks, chopped
- 4 cups vegetable broth
- 1 teaspoon cumin
- 1/2 teaspoon turmeric
- Salt and pepper to taste
- Whole wheat rolls for serving

Method:
1. Rinse the lentils and set aside.
2. In a pot, sauté chopped onion, carrots, and celery until softened.
3. Add rinsed lentils, vegetable broth, cumin, turmeric, salt, and pepper.
4. Bring to a boil, then reduce heat and let simmer until lentils are tender.
5. Use an immersion blender to partially blend the soup, leaving some texture.
6. Serve with whole wheat rolls.

Servings: 4
Preparation Time: 30 minutes

Hummus and Veggie Wrap:

Ingredients:

- Whole wheat tortilla wraps
- 1/2 cup hummus
- Sliced cucumbers, bell peppers, carrots, and other preferred veggies
- Baby spinach leaves

Method:

1. Lay out a whole wheat tortilla wrap.
2. Spread a generous layer of hummus on the wrap.
3. Layer sliced veggies and baby spinach leaves on top.
4. Roll up the wrap firmly, tucking in the sides as you go.

Servings: 1

Preparation Time: 10 minutes

Ingredients:

- 1 cup cooked brown rice
- 1 cup black beans, washed and drained
- 1 cup mixed veggies (corn, bell peppers, red onion, etc.)
- 1/4 cup salsa
- 1/4 cup chopped fresh cilantro
- Lime wedges for serving

Method:

1. In a bowl, combine cooked brown rice, black beans, mixed veggies, salsa, and chopped cilantro.
2. Toss well to mix all ingredients.
3. Serve with lime wedges for squeezing over the bowl.

Servings: 2

Preparation Time: 20 minutes

Caprese Salad with Balsamic Glaze:

Ingredients:
- Fresh mozzarella cheese, sliced
- Fresh tomatoes, sliced
- Fresh basil leaves
- Balsamic glaze
- Extra virgin olive oil
- Salt and pepper to taste

Method:
1. Arrange alternating slices of mozzarella, tomatoes, and basil leaves on a serving dish.
2. Drizzle with balsamic glaze and olive oil.
3. Season with salt and pepper.

Servings: 2
Preparation Time: 10 minutes

Roasted Vegetable and Couscous Medley:

Ingredients:

- 1 cup couscous
- 2 cups mixed roasted vegetables (zucchini, bell peppers, eggplant, etc.)
- 2 tablespoons olive oil
- 1 teaspoon dried herbs (thyme, rosemary, etc.)
- Salt and pepper to taste

Method:

1. Cook couscous according to package instructions.
2. Toss mixed roasted vegetables with olive oil, dried herbs, salt, and pepper.
3. Serve couscous topped with roasted vegetables.

Servings: 2

Preparation Time: 30 minutes

Stuffed Bell Peppers with Quinoa and Black Beans:

Ingredients:
- 2 large bell peppers
- 1 cup cooked quinoa
- 1/2 cup black beans, washed and drained
- 1/4 cup diced tomatoes
- 1/4 cup shredded cheese (optional)
- 1 teaspoon olive oil
- 1 teaspoon cumin
- Salt and pepper to taste

Method:
1. Preheat the oven to 375°F (190°C).
2. Cut the top part of bell peppers, deseed and remove membranes.
3. In a bowl, mix cooked quinoa, black beans, diced tomatoes, olive oil, cumin, salt, and pepper.
4. Tuck in the mixture into the bell peppers.
5. Put the stuffed peppers in a baking dish, top with shredded cheese if using.
6. Bake in the preheated oven for about 25-30 minutes or until peppers are tender.

Servings: 2
Preparation Time: 40 minutes

Spaghetti Squash with Marinara Sauce and Steamed Broccoli:

Ingredients:
- 1 medium spaghetti squash
- 1 cup marinara sauce
- 2 cups broccoli florets
- Olive oil
- Salt and pepper to taste
- Fresh basil leaves for garnish

Method:
1. Preheat the oven to 400°F (200°C).
2. Cut the spaghetti squash in half lengthwise, scoop out the seeds.
3. Drizzle the cut sides with olive oil, salt, and pepper.
4. Place the squash halves cut side down on a baking sheet.
5. Roast in the oven for about 30-40 minutes or until the squash strands can be easily separated with a fork.
6. Meanwhile, steam the broccoli until tender.
7. Once the squash is done, use a fork to scrape out the strands.
8. Serve the spaghetti squash topped with marinara sauce, steamed broccoli, and fresh basil leaves.

Servings: 2
Preparation Time: 50 minutes

Tofu and Vegetable Stir-Fry with Brown Rice:

Ingredients:

- 1 cup firm tofu, cubed
- 1 cup mixed vegetables (bell peppers, broccoli, carrots, etc.)
- 2 tablespoons soy sauce
- 1 tablespoon sesame oil
- 1 teaspoon minced garlic
- 1 cup cooked brown rice

Method:

1. Heat sesame oil in a pan over medium-high heat.
2. Add minced garlic and cubed tofu, sauté until tofu is golden brown.
3. Add mixed vegetables and stir-fry until slightly tender.
4. Pour in soy sauce and mix well.
5. Serve the tofu and vegetables over cooked brown rice.

Servings: 2

Preparation Time: 20 minutes

Mushroom and Spinach Stuffed Portobello Mushrooms:

Ingredients:
- 2 large Portobello mushrooms
- 1 cup chopped mushrooms
- 1 cup chopped spinach
- 1/4 cup shredded cheese (optional)
- 1 teaspoon olive oil
- 1 teaspoon balsamic vinegar
- Salt and pepper to taste

Method:
1. Preheat the oven to 375°F (190°C).
2. Take away the stems and gills from the Portobello mushrooms.
3. In a pan, heat olive oil and sauté chopped mushrooms and spinach until softened.
4. Remove from heat and stir in balsamic vinegar, salt, and pepper.
5. Fill the Portobello mushrooms with the sautéed mixture.
6. Top with shredded cheese if using.
7. Bake in the preheated oven for about 20 minutes or until mushrooms are tender.

Servings: 2
Preparation Time: 30 minutes

Roasted Vegetable and Chickpea Salad:

Ingredients:

- 2 cups mixed roasted vegetables (zucchini, bell peppers, red onion, etc.)
- 1 cup cooked chickpeas
- 2 cups mixed salad greens
- 1/4 cup crumbled feta cheese
- Balsamic vinaigrette dressing

Method:

1. Toss mixed roasted vegetables and chickpeas with a drizzle of olive oil, salt, and pepper.
2. Arrange the salad greens on a serving plate.
3. Top with the roasted vegetable and chickpea mixture.
4. Sprinkle crumbled feta cheese on top.
5. Drizzle balsamic vinaigrette dressing over the salad.

Servings: 2

Preparation Time: 30 minutes

Cauliflower and Lentil Curry with Whole Wheat Naan:

Ingredients:
- 1 cup cauliflower florets
- 1/2 cup cooked red or green lentils
- 1/2 cup diced tomatoes
- 1/2 cup diced onion
- 1 teaspoon minced ginger
- 1 teaspoon minced garlic
- 1 tablespoon curry powder
- 1/2 teaspoon cumin powder
- 1/2 teaspoon turmeric powder
- 1/2 teaspoon chili powder (adjust to taste)
- 1 cup coconut milk
- Salt and pepper to taste
- Fresh cilantro for garnish
- Whole wheat naan bread for serving

Method:
1. In a pan, sauté diced onion, minced ginger, and minced garlic until fragrant.
2. Add diced tomatoes and cook until softened.
3. Add curry powder, cumin powder, turmeric powder, and chili powder. Mix well.
4. Add cauliflower florets and cooked lentils, stirring to coat them with the spices.
5. Pour in coconut milk and bring to a simmer.
6. Let the curry simmer until the cauliflower is tender.
7. Season with salt and pepper.
8. Serve with whole wheat naan bread and garnish with fresh cilantro.

Servings: 2
Preparation Time: 40 minutes

Zucchini Noodles with Pesto and Cherry Tomatoes:

Ingredients:

- 2 medium zucchinis, spiralized into noodles
- 1 cup cherry tomatoes, halved
- 1/4 cup prepared pesto sauce
- Grated Parmesan cheese for garnish (optional)
- Fresh basil leaves for garnish

Method:

1. Heat a little olive oil in a pan over medium heat.
2. Add zucchini noodles and sauté for a few minutes until slightly softened.
3. Add halved cherry tomatoes and continue to sauté for another minute.
4. Remove from heat and toss with prepared pesto sauce.
5. Serve with a sprinkle of grated Parmesan cheese and fresh basil leaves.

Servings: 2

Preparation Time: 15 minutes

CHAPTER SIX: SNACK RECIPES

Carrot and Celery Sticks with Hummus:

Ingredients:

- Carrot sticks

- Celery sticks

- Hummus

Method:

1. Wash and peel the carrots if desired.

2. Cut carrots and celery into sticks.

3. Serve with a side of hummus for dipping.

Servings: 2

Preparation Time: 10 minutes

Greek Yogurt with Mixed Berries:

Ingredients:

- Greek yogurt

- Mixed berries (blueberries, strawberries, raspberries, etc.)

Method:

1. Spoon Greek yogurt into a bowl.

2. Top with mixed berries.

Servings: 1

Preparation Time: 5 minutes

Air-Popped Popcorn with Herbs and Spices:

Ingredients:

- Popcorn kernels

- Olive oil

- Herbs and spices (such as paprika, garlic powder, nutritional yeast, etc.)

Method:

1. Heat a pot over medium heat with a drizzle of olive oil.
2. Add popcorn kernels, cover with a lid, and shake occasionally.
3. Once popping slows down, remove from heat.
4. Toss with herbs and spices while still warm.

Servings: 2

Preparation Time: 10 minutes

Almonds and Walnuts Mix:

Ingredients:

- Almonds

- Walnuts

Method:

1. Mix almonds and walnuts in a bowl.

Servings: 2

Preparation Time: 2 minutes

Sliced Cucumber with Cottage Cheese:

Ingredients:

- Cucumber, sliced

- Cottage cheese

Method:

1. Wash and slice the cucumber.

2. Serve with a side of cottage cheese.

Servings: 1

Preparation Time: 5 minutes

Rice Cakes with Peanut Butter and Banana Slices:

Ingredients:

- Rice cakes

- Peanut butter

- Banana, sliced

Method:

1. Spread peanut butter on rice cakes.

2. Top with banana slices.

Servings: 2

Preparation Time: 5 minute

Veggie Chips (Baked Zucchini, Sweet Potato, or Kale):

Ingredients:

- Zucchini, sweet potato, or kale (or a mix of these)

- Olive oil

- Seasonings (salt, pepper, paprika, etc.)

Method:

1. Preheat the oven to 375°F (190°C).
2. Slice zucchini or sweet potato thinly, or tear kale into pieces.
3. Toss with olive oil and seasonings.
4. Arrange on a baking sheet and bake until crispy (around 15-20 minutes).

Servings: 2

Preparation Time: 20 minutes

CHAPTER SEVEN DESSERT RECIPES:

Mixed Berry Parfait with Greek Yogurt:

Ingredients:

- Greek yogurt

- Mixed berries (blueberries, strawberries, raspberries, etc.)

- Granola

- Honey or maple syrup

Method:

1. Layer Greek yogurt, mixed berries, and granola in a glass or bowl.
2. Drizzle with honey or maple syrup.

Servings: 1

Preparation Time: 5 minutes

Baked Apples with Cinnamon and Walnuts:

Ingredients:

- Apples (cored and halved)

- Cinnamon

- Chopped walnuts

- Honey

Method:

1. Preheat the oven to 350°F (175°C).
2. Place apple halves in a baking dish.
3. Sprinkle cinnamon and chopped walnuts on top.
4. Drizzle with honey.
5. Bake for about 20-25 minutes or until apples are tender.

Servings: 2

Preparation Time: 30 minutes

Chia Seed Pudding with Fresh Fruit:

Ingredients:

- Chia seeds

- Almond milk (or any milk you desire)

- Fresh fruit (berries, mango, kiwi, etc.)

- Honey or maple syrup

Method:

1. In a jar, mix chia seeds and almond milk.

2. Stir well and refrigerate overnight.

3. In the morning, layer chia pudding and fresh fruit in a glass.

4. Drizzle with honey or maple syrup.

Servings: 1

Preparation Time: 5 minutes (plus overnight refrigeration)

Dark Chocolate-Dipped Strawberries:

Ingredients:

- Fresh strawberries

- Dark chocolate (70% cocoa or higher)

- Chopped nuts (optional)

Method:

1. Wash and dry the strawberries.
2. Melt dark chocolate in a microwave or double boiler.
3. Dip each strawberry in the melted chocolate, allowing excess to drip off.
4. Place on a parchment-lined tray.
5. If using, sprinkle chopped nuts on the chocolate.
6. Let the chocolate set before serving.

Servings: Varies

Preparation Time: 15 minutes

Mango Sorbet with Mint Leaves:

Ingredients:

- Ripe mangoes, peeled and diced

- Fresh mint leaves

- Lime juice

- Honey or agave syrup (optional)

Method:

1. Blend diced mangoes, fresh mint leaves, and a squeeze of lime juice until smooth.

2. Taste and add honey or agave syrup if needed for sweetness.

3. Pour the ready-made mixture into a shallow container and freeze.

4. Once frozen, scoop and serve.

Servings: Varies

Preparation Time: 10 minutes (plus freezing time)

Oatmeal Raisin Cookies

(Using whole wheat flour and less sugar):

Ingredients:
- Whole wheat flour
- Rolled oats
- Baking powder
- Cinnamon
- Raisins
- Coconut oil or butter
- Egg
- Honey or maple syrup

Method:
1. Preheat the oven to 350°F (175°C).
2. In a bowl, mix whole wheat flour, rolled oats, baking powder, and cinnamon.
3. In another bowl, whisk together melted coconut oil or butter, egg, and honey or maple syrup.
4. Mix the wet and dry ingredients, then fold in raisins.
5. Scoop dough onto a baking sheet and flatten each cookie.
6. Bake for about 10-12 minutes or until cookies are golden.

Servings: Varies
Preparation Time: 25 minutes

Fruit Salad with Honey-Lime Drizzle:

Ingredients:

- Mixed fresh fruits (melon, berries, pineapple, kiwi, etc.)

- Honey

- Lime juice

- Fresh mint leaves (optional)

Method:

1. Wash, peel, and chop the fresh fruits.
2. In a bowl, whisk together honey and lime juice for the drizzle.
3. Toss the chopped fruits with the honey-lime drizzle.
4. Garnish with fresh mint leaves if desired.

Servings: Varies

Preparation Time: 15 minutes

Green Power Smoothie with Spinach and Banana:

Ingredients:

- 1 cup spinach leaves
- 1 ripe banana
- 1/2 cup Greek yogurt
- 1/2 cup almond milk
- 1 tablespoon chia seeds (optional)
- Honey or maple syrup (optional)

Method:

1. Blend spinach, banana, Greek yogurt, almond milk, and chia seeds (if using) until smooth.
2. Taste and add honey or maple syrup if desired.
3. Pour into a glass and enjoy.

Servings: 1

Preparation Time: 5 minutes

Berry Blast Smoothie with Mixed Berries and Almond Milk:

Ingredients:

- 1 cup mixed berries (blueberries, strawberries, raspberries, etc.)
- 1/2 cup almond milk
- 1/2 cup Greek yogurt
- 1 tablespoon honey or agave syrup

Method:

1. Blend mixed berries, almond milk, Greek yogurt, and honey or agave syrup until smooth.
2. Pour into a glass and serve.

Servings: 1

Preparation Time: 5 minutes

Tropical Paradise Smoothie with Pineapple, Mango, and Coconut Water:

Ingredients:

- 1 cup diced pineapple
- 1/2 cup diced mango
- 1/2 cup coconut water
- 1/2 cup Greek yogurt
- Lime juice (optional)
- Honey or agave syrup (optional)

Method:

1. Blend pineapple, mango, coconut water, Greek yogurt, and a squeeze of lime juice (if using) until smooth.
2. Taste and add honey or agave syrup if desired.
3. Pour into a glass and enjoy.

Servings: 1
Preparation Time: 5 minutes

Creamy Avocado Smoothie with Lime and Honey:

Ingredients:
- 1/2 ripe avocado
- 1/2 cup Greek yogurt
- Juice of 1 lime
- 1 tablespoon honey or agave syrup
- 1/2 cup almond milk

Method:
1. Blend avocado, Greek yogurt, lime juice, honey or agave syrup, and almond milk until creamy.
2. Pour into a glass and serve.

Servings: 1

Preparation Time: 5 minutes

Peanut Butter Banana Smoothie with Greek Yogurt:

Ingredients:

- 1 ripe banana
- 1 tablespoon peanut butter
- 1/2 cup Greek yogurt
- 1/2 cup almond milk
- Honey or agave syrup (optional)

Method:

1. Blend banana, peanut butter, Greek yogurt, almond milk, and honey or agave syrup until smooth.
2. Pour into a glass and enjoy.

Servings: 1

Preparation Time: 5 minutes

Cucumber Mint Cooler Smoothie:

Ingredients:

- 1 cucumber, peeled and diced
- Handful of fresh mint leaves
- 1/2 cup coconut water
- Juice of 1 lime
- Honey or agave syrup (optional)

Method:

1. Blend cucumber, mint leaves, coconut water, lime juice, and honey or agave syrup until smooth.
2. Pour into a glass and serve.

Servings: 1

Preparation Time: 5 minutes

Oatmeal and Almond Smoothie with Dates and Cinnamon:

Ingredients:

- 1/4 cup rolled oats
- 2 tablespoons chopped almonds
- 2-3 pitted dates
- 1/2 teaspoon cinnamon
- 1/2 cup almond milk
- 1/2 cup Greek yogurt

Method:

1. Blend rolled oats, chopped almonds, pitted dates, cinnamon, almond milk, and Greek yogurt until smooth.
2. Pour into a glass and enjoy.

Servings: 1

Preparation Time: 5 minutes

CONCLUSION

As you reach the final pages of the Vegetarian DASH Diet cookbook, you've not only journeyed through a myriad of flavors and dishes but also embarked on a path towards vibrant health and holistic well-being. The culmination of vegetarian ingenuity and DASH principles has brought you to a place where every meal is a symphony of nourishment, every bite a testament to your commitment to your health.

But this isn't the end; rather, it's a new beginning. Armed with a repertoire of recipes that tantalize your taste buds and fortify your health, you're now equipped to continue this culinary adventure in your own kitchen. The recipes within these pages are meant to inspire your creativity, encouraging you to tweak, experiment, and infuse your personal touch into each dish.

As you move forward, remember that the Vegetarian DASH Diet isn't just a temporary dietary shift; it's a lifestyle that embraces the harmony between your body's needs and your taste preferences. Whether you're cooking for yourself, your family, or your friends, the principles you've gained from this cookbook will remain invaluable companions on your journey to optimal health.

In a world where dietary choices can seem overwhelming, you've embraced a path that radiates balance and wellness. The Vegetarian DASH Diet cookbook isn't just a collection of recipes; it's a testament to your dedication to a healthier and more vibrant you. So, go forth with confidence, armed with spatula and skillet, ready to create meals that are not only delicious but also transformative. As you savor each dish, remember that you're nurturing not only your body but also your spirit, one bite at a time.

Thank you for joining us on this delectable journey of flavors, discovery, and well-being. May your kitchen forever be a canvas where health and taste intertwine, and may your life be seasoned with the joy that comes from taking charge of your health in the most delightful way possible. Here's to a future filled with scrumptious meals, boundless vitality, and the radiant glow that stems from within – all courtesy of the Vegetarian DASH Diet.

Bon appétit and cheers to a healthier, happier you!

Printed in Great Britain
by Amazon

46083511R00046